More Praise for *Tender Headed*

"'I can attest that men learn to play men from men still learning.' In Olatunde Osinaike's *Tender Headed*, we find a contemplative, earnest young man seriously engaged with inherited notions of masculinity and 'Blackness,' one who examines the problems, perils, and pleasures of each, and means to make sense of it all. This alone would make Osinaike's debut collection a worthwhile read, but what sets it apart from most of what passes for socially engaged 'poetry' nowadays is that Osinaike is not relying on The Project to do the heavy lifting. Rather, he is writing actual poems. Inventive, musical, and surprising poems. Imagine Terrance Hayes and Ishion Hutchinson had a baby, and said baby stepped to a podium rocking an MF Doom mask. Now imagine this masked man with something serious to say. *Tender Headed* is fresh, ferocious, and sets a high bar for whichever bars are brought next to the circle. To quote Osinaike himself, when 'he jumps into the cypher with the homies, he sings.'"

—**John Murillo**, award-winning author of *Kontemporary Amerikan Poetry*

"Olatunde Osinaike is an oracle, and *Tender Headed* is his holy, foretelling text. These poems ask us to 'pivot [our] necks to scan what has been done,' then fix our eyes ahead on a Black coming-of-age, a Black coming-of-risk. With precise linguistic cleverness, Osinaike shapes, mangles, and unearths gospels to smoothen the serrated edges of masculinity. What's cultivated in this resistance is space for our breathing, space for our being. *Tender Headed* annihilates the lie of a singular Black male identity. Lucky for us, rather than running from its falsehood, Osinaike decides to 'make [his] living as a truth teller.'"

—**Courtney Faye Taylor**, author of *Concentrate*, winner of the Cave Canem Poetry Prize

"*Tender Headed* is a simmering and sensitive offering from a poet of great promise. These poems sing of a writer seeking to make sense of the masculinity we've been handed from a sick society. In these poems we see a writer looking through the varied lenses of hip-hop, hallelujahs, and hair grease in order to reach towards something akin to healing. This is a special book from an exciting voice."

—**Nate Marshall**, award-winning author of *Finna*

"*Tender Headed* is a tour de force exploration, to be sure, of Black vulnerability—with its etymological roots in how we wear our wounds—but also, critically, a certain vision of Black overcoming and abundance. Throughout this collection, we are not only surviving, but celebrating. We are irreducibly alive. For this breadth of vision and daring intervention alone, Olatunde Osinaike's luminous debut merits praise. But there's more. This poet has a truly remarkable ear, and a refreshing sense of assuredness in the range of his voice. He 'cannot bury the music.' He understands that poems are social occasions; that they find new life once given over to the air. And there is air everywhere in this boundless book: in breath, in ascension, in song."
—**Joshua Bennett**, award-winning author of *The Sobbing School*

"There is a dexterity it takes to weave through the mundane and make it feel radical, to break normality over itself until it is no longer something of easy comfort, and Olatunde Osinaike shows this off in his debut collection. *Tender Headed* deftly uses contemporary language as a form unto itself—a series of humming vignettes that move with a kinetic sharpness that rarely slow to catch their breath. At one point, Osinaike writes, 'I made a mannerism out of faith,' and it is clear that there is a longing for answers that will not come easy, birthed from questions many writers wouldn't have the fortification to ask. Osinaike's confidence in the movement between styles, but the vulnerability in the lens he allows us to view the world through makes for a complicated negotiation between the brick/mortar of the language and serenity of his voice. *Tender Headed* is a pleading, a prayer shared with a stranger, a reluctant fist resting upon your shoulder that asks, demands, insists on your attention."
—**William Evans**, author of *We Inherit What the Fires Left*

"The poems in *Tender Headed* span a variation of volume, tone, and pitch. They beg to answer the question of what it means to be a Black man not only surviving, but living: 'How does one look for a fight when it is already in you?' To the speaker, language is a tool of delight and discovery, weaving in and out of sonic and idiomatic play. And everything is biblical, from the barbershop to the gas station to Grandma's house. Through praise and parables, spells and invention, *Tender Headed* challenges and captivates. It blooms beyond the page, strong in all its tenderness: 'Oh I can be such a mess when the world lets me. Gorgeous / with sympathy.'"
—**Diannely Antigua**, author of *Ugly Music*, winner of the Whiting Award

TEN DER HEA DED

OLATUNDE OSINAIKE

NATIONAL POETRY SERIES WINNER • SELECTED BY CAMILLE RANKINE

BROOKLYN, NEW YORK

The National Poetry Series was established in 1978 to ensure the publication of five collections of poetry annually through five participating publishers. The Series is funded annually by Amazon Literary Partnership, William Geoffrey Beattie, the Gettinger Family Foundation, Bruce Gibney, HarperCollins Publishers, the Stephen and Tabitha King Foundation, Padma Lakshmi, Lannan Foundation, Newman's Own Foundation, Anna and Olafur Olafsson, Penguin Random House, the Poetry Foundation, Amy Tan and Louis DeMattei, Amor Towles, Elise and Steven Trulaske, and the National Poetry Series Board of Directors.

———

Published by Akashic Books
©2023 Olatunde Osinaike

ISBN: 978-1-63614-141-1
Library of Congress Control Number: 2023933947

All rights reserved
First printing

Akashic Books
Brooklyn, New York
Instagram, Twitter, Facebook: AkashicBooks
E-mail: info@akashicbooks.com
Website: www.akashicbooks.com

for Ayo and Kunmi

To name something
is to wait for it
in the place
you think
it will pass.

Amiri Baraka

TABLE OF CONTENTS

FORTE

PREFACE

In *Tender Headed*, Olatunde Osinaike asks the question: what makes a man, and what makes a man like me? As he interrogates the inner and outer workings of masculinity in all its sharp and tender parts, and the way a Black man meets the world, his poems strut and duck and weave across their pages. These poems unpack the ingredients of being and make a meal of language. They relish every word, every sound, every syllable. Their music is the sugar that makes us take our medicine, but their beauty refuses to be disguise. They disturb the peace while asking: whose peace?

The poems are playful, not playing. They pulse and spin and push us forward, never carry us away. Even as we dance along, we never close our eyes. This work is nimble. A two-step on a tightwire. *Tender Headed* grooves and shines, holds us wide awake and mesmerized.

—Camille Rankine, author of *Incorrect Merciful Impulses*

MEN LIKE ME

Boys.   Will be boys. Manly. Slick. Elbow grease. Baritones. Singing low. Unruly. Higher than a hierarchy. Inherit. Plausible deniability. Disorder. Bachelors and awful apostles. Dark knights. Concaved like a character arc. Compensate. Compensation. Deafen a suffrage. Sulk. Storm sellers. The fragrance of kingdoms. Ladybug and don't believe much in luck. Believe in overstaying a welcome. Will name anything after us. Detention centers and muscle cars. Squad. Thumbed-through classifieds. Flashing lights. Shock value. Slide hands in the slow close of an elevator door. Door stoppers. Stop things. Won't. Will rep the rhetorical like it's the home team. Shoot the shot to blame the angle. Blame things. See floral print and scurry. See flowers like flowers hold both water and scent. Sent some heaven-sent a good morning text this week. Gossip but call that barbershop talk. Double meaning. Deprecating. Duffel bag crazy. Colonialize. Call that authority. Monopolize until it's good guise. Tough guise. All of the above. Treat all we touch like tungsten. Can't temper anything. Love a melting point. Get physical. Have a problem with the word *no*. Yes men. Have more than *just a problem with* the word *no*. Antsy with violence. Prefer a seat or stall between us and another. Stick up for and subjugated to nothing. Jog memories for fun. Jog freely at night. Night and day. Interrogate. Bastard. Blue everything. Culture coercion. Hate to admit it. With tailored suits. Soot and tie. Checker. Call it chess. Don't call it *control*. Call it. Like a time of death. A flat tire. Said with our chests. Repeat what's been said before but in a tone society loves. Hate being adjacent to the action. Hate. Keep that. Invest. Keep that. In hotbeds and chitchat. Men of the house. Our own men. Might not start it, but will end it. Love when we aren't followed or replaced. Love having the last word so we take it wherever we go. Front lines. Confessional booths. Prenups. Shotgun weddings. *Law & Order* reruns. Boardrooms. Proms. Distilleries. Salary negotiations. Horror films. Oval offices. On air.

TENOR

Been living in an idea, an idea from another man's mind
—Frank Ocean

ON DEEP CONDITIONING

August, and the boy wells up with pride like the city bird. His first love was not a fade, but instead a 'fro. And like the fastest in the kingdom, he can see the forest from the trees, the plot from the wishful thinking. When he is asked what he wants, he spots the command strips on the wall, the speckled plaster of which does not disturb him in the way the twists and locks do. It is a terrible year for appeal and it isn't that they are unkept, but that sometime before he swung the tempered glass of the exit open, the world had already convinced him what was his to keep.

\\\

A few known facts about that bird. They are known to live on skyscrapers in the municipal. The species' name most closely translates to *wanderer*. They thrive in the open. And the boy cares little as you do for these cues. Daily, he refuses them and watches chance broadcasts on blue jays. But the tree branches in the boy's neighborhood have all fallen. The boy expressly misses one letter whenever he spells out the word *accommodate*. The boy is in the other room lobbying his lungs into a quintessential r&b'd *hold me down*. The boy does not have braids, has never had braids, but admires the effect they have in music videos. The boy gets one of his ears pierced on a whim at a booth in the mall. It is the right one. By the time he is in the car, he has been questioned by loved ones and strangers. He is told the right one is seen as *the wrong one* and he would be remiss to have it if he doesn't want to be seen in *that way*. The piercing closed by year's end. It is hot and infected.

\\\

The boy goes years without hearing a bedtime story but won't go mere weeks without the touch of the blade on the tip of a clipper. Every time the boy heads into the shop, there are as many women waiting as there are men. Every time the boy sees a woman barber, he observes the aversion. There are half of half as many men willing to sit in the woman's chair. The boy knows how the men feel about women there by the peculiar quell of complaints launched when they are present compared to when they are absent. *If women are difficult, then what are we?* the boy grieves as he thinks of the kinks of conflating. For all other animals, we are content in our calling their skin *hide*. But for us, it is described by the many violences we have not hidden from. For us, it is the charm of virility. The boy palms the mirror and pivots his neck to scan what has been done. He gripes with his ends splattered like small clouds across the floor. Brushes his roots despite his sense of breakage.

ARS POETICA

Does soft it make
the shins of a child

when thick skin is
not a question of

susceptibility or blistering?
That during their brief

time in this hemisphere,
they are thankful that

they haven't been
jumped. That they can

flaunt their wingspan
at all is something to be

admired and not frantic
about. Look out the window

and please tell me where
you don't see the after-

math of heliotherapy.
Where is it exactly that

you enjoy being judged
as stiff as the larynx

of a tight chest. This
life of first impressions,

of shakes ranked by
their unyielding grip.

Every muscle I am aware of
is best while at rest.

AN INCONVENIENCE

Men lay tarp over a grassy field but won't dare
       touch a cloth over a dead torso at the risk
of tampering a scene. Men shave the scalp
      of another before they abandon that body

and say this, this resembles clemency. I do my job
      the same as any man with a need to provide
      for his need to provide. Allegiant to the lure,
immune to the plea. And on the off occasion I reach out

      to someone with texts that trapeze tone
      like treble, I perform everything in my own power
      to not double up as if to not veto my own ego
and call them stuck up for it. I took a pencil

      into my hand this afternoon. Haven't put
it down since I haven't quite put into words
      the haggling of my heart. Stubborn dream
seizing up between what has and what needs

      to be. I sat down thinking of inconvenience
and this poem, unfazed by its brief brave,
went out of its own way to rumble about
the saddest quo. My callous woes, my avid

      habits to banish what does not suit me.
      I used to be a 44" husky and now I despise
anything which doesn't lend me enough room
      to try on what I shall dispose of.

Hello, my name has been said. Blessed, my color
        is forest green, and my pet peeves all
revolve around me, repeating myself. A bit more
        about me is that I am a hypocrite,

a salutatorian, a romantic with his tag inside out.
        Taught to fish by men who kiss
their wrists at the free throw line. What I do,
a routine best left up in the air.

ETYMOLOGY OF SIMP

Long ago, a boy surveys the series of
of a woman, towels draped across the
and if skin operates within the same
the same boy offers a compliment on
This is the first time he is told this by
world all over again—only this time

or that the other boy wants them both
or maybe they were taught inversely or
stopped and meant to say *bless you.*
fret over the little things. So when
one out for his. When he mentions

boys back in third period, they laugh.
or with him, he plays it off to ensure
the fact that he's well aware of what
still does not know why the practice

When the music video shows the girl
to impress her, he blushes as well.
time there's enough eye contact and

watching intently. There's plenty of
the question of who will wear them
The very next time he jumps into

heads that swivel toward the direction
base of her neck as he marvels magnetism
guidelines. In what feels like years later,
his brother's outerwear and is told *pause.*
another boy and he wonders about the
he thinks maybe the pause is mistaken,

to reflect on what hasn't been said yet,
honest to god he just assumed his heart
At the banquet, it was thought polite to
their mothers approach their seats, he pulls
his highlights from etiquette to the other

When it is not clear whether it is at him
it's with. He does things like leave out
nail polish looks like and does or that he
of averting is too much to ask of himself.

blushing at the guy dancing on the street
He's still not sure why but at least this
dialogue that even the sun's flushed and

pants to go around, so much so that
in their relationship never comes up.
the cypher with the homies, he sings.

SMALL DEVOTIONALS

after Ladan Osman

Blessed insurance, Jesus is mine. That used to be my favorite
possession. I kept it tucked in my back pocket for
special occasions. Like this here. Like this, tiered.

Payback is a great-grandmother. And I asked for answers,
when reason had no use there. I didn't know when
to stop. *Raising my labor all the day long.* Beaten

down, I clean the tub. After a while, the dirt dips down
the drain but it was not always this way. I used to
not grow any hair at all and for that I was called

young. Now I shed so much hair, you would've thought
I was Samson livid with the ploy of liability.
Filled with his goodness, washed in his love.

///

The midday sermon was about Isaac. There were three
takeaways but I only recall that he didn't know what
he didn't know. You could be heading to your own

sacrifice, saliva as a last supper. *Take me to the water to be
chastised.* The bare minimum of dignity. Privilege:
imploring a kind of quality of life that remains

after affliction. Antonyms against the hymned hearts.
None but the nicest shall behave in the way we assume
they should. I make the mistake of making

a living as a truth teller. But I know no more than you,
or you, or you. At what point do you say enough?
Gonna gray here no longer, I decide for myself.

///

Across the grove, we are groans away from an ode to sleeping
in, crud resting in the eye at face value. I need you and
you've seen me. At this point, love might be the only

thing that saves us. I make us breakfast with what we
have in the fridge. It's not much but it'll do for now.
At the cross, at the cross where I first caught the light.

It'll hold us over. Until we can grab delivery and get
saved again. Beneath the shower head. Before
dinner, *where the verdicts of my heart rolled away.*

It was there by faith I redeemed my might. There, there
I glared for too long like a staring contest with
the sun. I still see you when I close my eyes.

THE THIRD DEGREE

So help me soft spot in my ego, tears for the times I have downplayed the lateral to liminal. Safe spaces to punctuate what I am vested in and yesteryear's posturing in the name of hindsight. There are questions that need answers and then there are questions that need, tenets like drills left rhetorical. There is wanting to be grown, and then, phoning a friend. Cliff Notes paraphrased from cliffs. Beating around bushes afire. No one desires to be burned. Everything within shouting distance is an emergency contact. I, like everyone, wanting to be made whole by sight.

\ \ \

So help me help *the blood that gives me strength*, help the spared rods and my frailty left to spoil, help my restraint like a nephew might. So help me keep count of the times I have counted myself lucky, opting to be remembered by minute remnants: lint, tentative love, my borrowed time. There has always been a divide between discard and touch, how hazmat suits beget quarantine, become the rate at which ache releases like paramedics seething to mend, like sprinklers going off in the night.

\ \ \

So help me witness protection, I am not my conviction. I am in danger of considering only the wrongs as if in a plea bargain. Soon someone shall take what I see for what I shall say. Soon what leaves will indulge what will come back and I know this by the scabs along my lining. Fact is I stayed in the chair. Fact is, during the few times I took kindness for weakness, I said please. I had manners. I knew right from rite.

MERCY, MERCY ME

To no one's surprise, I'm not a betting man. What, with my manner thin, my tastes
    doctored,
my heart safe—I am as good as any last Ash Wednesday, as elusive as any double
    negative.
Domains of dominoes and mustard seeds undone on my tongue. As if out of a parable,

I was once found in the South, studying the aviation of snowflakes, how even in
    the darkness
they can melt midflight. I was once told *try me*. Then to speak it into existence.
    But I am
clumsy. Whatever it was I do not recall. The funny things flaws become: shambles,

soliloquy, spiritual. It was the same way I learned how to use *might could* in a sen-
    tence. And to
this day I haven't let go of how I could taunt a scythe with nothing more than
    some dirt
and my brave lips. Oh, I can be such a mess when this world lets me. Gorgeous

with sympathy. Nimble as an imperative. I submit because I care, too. Because I
    cannot trade
away this audacity. Because so much can happen in a week. A horse loses a race.
    A race
loses its culture. A culture loses its place. A place loses its mothers. Mothers lose

their babies. Babies lose their wonder. If you ask me how I shall stay fed until the
    next first
of the month, I would tell you I already have a full-time job. If you ask what will
    keep

me sane, I would want you to know I take vacation seriously like every good

love story. Try me. In a game of charades where *making a snow angel* is as heaven-
   ly as it sounds.
I can't even romanticize this part. The thankless credential of raising a body
from the dead. That it might could be yours. How I've filled this life

with disbelief in between. Lord, I'm not actually sure it's fair
of me to assume you know where all the time goes.

CONCERNING SOCIAL SECURITY

after Yona Harvey

Is it so wrong of me to ask for common ground
in this calculated gamut of a world? Nine digits to tell

me that I am special, and ten digits to show
me that I am within reach. I did bottle service

once to feel alive. What can I say? The lights
did what they came to do. Left me wanting more.

Friday night and the club is thick with chasers.
Friday night, furtive and fervent. I was once fond

of this fail-safe. Escaped. As though free is as free
does but who knows anymore. *What gives*

says the guys lined up beside me for a twenty-
dollar cover. It seems they've been waiting

forever and can wait awhile longer. For the love of
taking, we've been trained. *It's just business*, I tell myself

as I dip into a pocket and thumb up the card of a lawyer
I keep *just* in case. The way *just* becomes filler, pulp

in the eleventh hour. In my throat I skirt the line,
and trouble up a hum of *the way we do the things we do*.

VERISIMILITUDE

Fellas, do you feel me when I say
she need not
be a daughter, an example,
or the marvel

of a model citizen? Fellas,
is it just me
or do we deflect in times
we ought to cut

the decoys fabricated beneath
our charm?
On her shoe rack, Converses
and glass slippers

she picked out for herself.
Fellas,
are we spoiled stiff
or spoiled

in our willful reluctance to make
eye contact
with delight. Fellas, what does it
mean to you

to *be the bigger man?* I haven't
figured it out
for myself, so I took a chance
to hold water

and it overflowed, being bigger than
my pampered
rapport, said the poet in me
that falters

when he thinks he can simulate
submission
in this poem and catch
slack

because of it. Can hardly
refer
to my first person without release,
without my weak

bleak and unleashed to protect
the pact
I made with the boy. An oath
to never

go to bed angry so I stayed up
all the day
to overcompensate like only I
know how.

Fellas, what does it matter
the articles
on the body of another when
we

have the loneliest grasp of
revealing
the real. *It takes one to know*
one

but I latch onto the lozenge
in my palm
like it can quench my meaning,
my pocket

full of odes that might corrode
my mode.
Fellas, I don't call you my dawgs
to heal,

I call you my dawgs because I'd
like
to see you open up, the way
two

thumbs can point up in the midst
of something we call war
when really

we're mid-dap. You feel me?

THERE IS NO I IN DENIAL

Somebody tell the boy *talk is cheap* before I show him how we get down. Loaded
   statements.
*You supposed to wear white on first Sundays. The male gaze runs in our family. Check
   yourself*

before you wreck your selective memory. Almost doesn't count on most days,
but today it will. And so while I could sit here and tell the boy reasons

why practice makes perfect, I'd rather show him.
I pick up a remote and turn his two eyes toward

the screen while I liaise the two of mine toward complicity. There's a scene in *A
   Different World*
where Dwayne demands the prenuptial glance of a former lover. We both stare and
   smile.

This must be how we stage the gesture. Blur the jealousy. Play the role perfect
as practice might suggest so in the end we all know how it must go.

With a certainty that levels a meet cute, with an affection
we can twist into, with an affirmation

we could get misty from. No matter how I swing it, command is a distinction of pitch.
It's no surprise the suited men followed suit. I have desired a sacrifice like that,

something we take a swig of and spit out when bitter. I might have to tell
the boy a truth. That what we've seen might be considered

method acting, but this is how some of us
men learn romance. And luckily

for the boy and me, we were given tu-
lips so we could talk about it.

I KNOW THE HUSTLE SO WELL

You know I just need to be around some love, b
—Money Making Mitch

Twenty on pump three as I stare down
a guy exhibiting a gray that could date
him heirloomed as Moses—a man

with nothing left to say. That part,
like his staff or my clippers underneath
a drab sink, condoned by bro code.

Judas was grown, I am in my mid-
twenties. With my canteen raised
fractions as high, I wonder what it

must be to stand in a field that could
easily be a drop zone. We are living in
a time of prerogatives, a city of

exaggerations headed southbound.
But first, I need to get my tires
rotated, my oil changed, and refill

my gas since my tank is three-quarters of
the way to empty. Grabbing a snack,
attempting to extinguish the fumes

of my hunger, I notice him to my left.
A pack of Newports he cots in his right
while he smashes his hand into

its back to shake loose his urge to
get free. But he's right. Come to think
of it, has a word ever been adequate?

BRIEF NOTES ON GHOSTWRITING

I should start by saying I'm frightfully aware of how easy it is to *catch a body* these days or rather how normal it may seem I am told this in all the top hits the freestyles & interviews after there's no clear-cut way to be certain whose body is being caught & whose voice is lobbying on the hook line & since I know at the very least that my chest is puffed out at the moment & that it doesn't take much to blow hot air & a few minutes prior I cut the safety off while I merged lanes & I threw my head back peeking out the window for whomever wants the strap & the holes & the blood it won't be mine you should know by now this is all for you your mouth cloaking these words in a familiar & arraigned spit now my pen silent too my boo-lean logic of a bid if I confess then somebody is getting locked up & if I don't it still won't be me what's more precious than my narratives with my tone I can invert a sight line send you south I got a discography full of outros & what do I get in return I'll tell you I'll show you royalties euphemisms confidentiality & your head nodding to the stories I've lived & I've lived long enough to tell the truth any echo can sound like me with the right reflection the human ear can barely distinguish an echo from the original melody sung with the perfect amount of delay so spare me who you'd summon to the séance & instead tell me you feel right at home shoot it's that simple what's done in the dark shall be ethical shall come to be commerce then commercial on your tongue look here I already got a rough draft with your name on it

ON SIGHT

We promise,
where I'm from,

to lay hands

on the harsh hero.
We bond over

shared distrusts,

the rigged devils
soldiered onto

our traps

until we flesh out
the outlets of our

guaranteed.

For power, we strip
and slow

to anger.

Dressed to diss
the dismal

and done so,

with a dollar menu
deferred until

triumph

presents a worthy
stench. Fuming

from this tedious game

of freeze tag.
And my

growth spurt

back in the tenth
has done nothing

to correct this

obnoxious reach.
So it's *on sight*

for you.

Enough with
the stalling,

sticks and stones.

Never have I ever
been indecisive,

or nearsighted at that.

LESSONS FROM COOLEY HIGH

Hesitation, like that at the top
of a key, at the thought of bringing
a black child into a world that won't know
how to score them. And later, baby fever.
Preach, I felt you knew poetry better
than I do because you felt poetry

before I could. Preach, I too haven't
come up with the right lie yet. My false
equivalence. You recite Benton as if there
is no harbor to your windpipe, no harpoon
whistling. Toward your heaven, only girls
you adore and I want to get there

but I break toward the train tracks,
Cochise in his all-city letterman lying
there despite his reputation. He was
supposed to make it out, and now
he's stuck like my zipper which bit off
more than it can chew. To make it home,

this winter evening, I practically skated
on ice as I reminisced the game of pickup
that broke my fall. Preach, is it too late
to darling our youth? To get back to sleep?
Binge-watching the block, I can see myself
in each cheap thrill, every two-point turn.

TREMOLO

… and there's been so many things a Caucasian person said I couldn't do. Get good credit. Buy a house in an urban city. So many things—"you can't do that"—whether it's from afar or close up. So if I say this is my word, let me have this one word, please let me have that word.
—Kendrick Lamar Duckworth

TRILL

won't be an acquittal today won't be a strikethrough won't be an excerpt won't
be a subdominant chord won't be dissonant won't be in Hidden Hills won't be
a think piece won't be a throwback won't be sagging won't be objectification
won't be worldstar won't be a cold front won't be lines drawn in the grains
in the gain after the sun settles and sandcastles have dwindled near newer
horizons won't be a gram won't be a loose canon it won't be *less of a man* won't
be less won't be a stash that big screens have shown the black man to be hid-
ing won't be a black man hidden won't be black men hiding behind their own
tongues won't be untrue won't be leaning onto the hood of an impala won't
be hum-silent and running like an engine it won't be clean on the inside it won't
be clean on the outside won't be shots fired won't be triage won't be on the
front pages won't be a dry run won't be conditional won't be a clause won't be
overlooked like the lower third of a news ticker won't be news won't be over
won't be over heat won't be heat waved won't be a doubt while listening to
TLC's greatest hits won't be without house music won't be house arrest won't
be a caress without consent won't be followed by stunted breathing or shallow
expectations won't be a spitting image won't be spit won't be the spit of a verse
won't be the change of a topic to avoid the topic won't be veins pushing up
through skin to kiss the sky a prayer by proxy it won't be fade-catching it won't
be a shot in the dark it won't be won't be an absence of kin or a ship we haven't
emerged from already won't be a new era if you mean what strip of sweat I
have peeled from my forehead after swag surfing won't be a delta if you mean
a way and a will for a slave and a crop and away to the wash and go my dear-
est done did this morning it won't be done if what you mean is what I think
it won't be finishing up it won't be finished won't be to finish won't be what
makes you think I won't be what makes it

I DON'T GET DROPPED, I DROP THE LABEL

I know what won't hold me by the lot of mouths that call me out of my name. So do it. Call me out of it so I can say it ain't so. So you know that I know you know I'm done pretending. It's all good. Allow me to reintroduce myself. Oasis. Haven. Son of a sanctuary. I smile sincere with my eyes squinted so I subtract. What I can't see are the skeptics. They reserved the septic for me. Never that. There's more to me and my clique than acrylic and icebreakers. Understand the never-ending product placement incited by our tongues. Who even has time for the preheat of an oven? Who among our zephyr spread across brownstones require training wheels? We've worn farewells in the thick of home-video marathons. We've worn em-dashes of eye black across our cheeks in the name of good sportsmanship. My contemporaries with cola-caked nickels in the cup holder as they pull up to the window sovereign. Superfood or fast food still fed frequent. The joy of Lent we make stretch until next paycheck. The seltzer we've nixed. The steeze we've stipulated. Shout-out to my people who are without middle names as if *to be continued* is what they are tethered to. This is for my homies who have headed a household without a chaperone. I have who looks like me at every vigil. With floor seats. In heavy rotation. Bouncing in sync to basslines as if in the gather before a round of double dutch. We not even in this for the clout. I count the amount of times me and mine have eliminated the need for name tags. When I take one I feel sorry for whomever has it twisted. Think *as soon as I put this on,*

I put this on the sky.

MAKE ROOM

Per the brake check.
Plate the paycheck.
Vet the cassette.

Unwind the writhing.
Beneath the blanket.
Empty the dishwasher.

Fatten the gut.
Baffle the belief.
Pad the corridor.

Tag the coupons.
Complex the loft.
Soften the tone.

Elegant the groove.
Elude the contract.
Expose the knuckle.

Anchor the thank.
Embellish the blues.
Ante the tendency.

Prime the prone.
Contend the yes.
Extend the bridge.

Candid the doing.
The good lord taketh.
The breath we loosen.

Check the driveway.
Choose the drive-in.
Find the live kin.

Unpack the trauma.
Empty the bladder.
Tidy the gutter.

Sweeten the raffle.
Reckon the grief.
Debrick the wall.

Pawn the futon.
Vacant the half bath.
Detach the known.

Remove the remorse.
Refuse the fuse.
Dispose the smock.

Muddy the swank.
Ample the view.
Boost the belonging.

Slick the chime.
Square the yet.
Above the bunker.

Control the portion.
Away to shorten.
The breath we hoarding.

ESCALATOR TALK

is made up.
awe. My mind
Shock and grand
us human with ache.
felt like, sharp as it harps
character but that's what this
one is watching. I haven't broken
say character is who you are when no
This is the way injustice happens as they
still hasn't come. They have indicted no one.
prayers. Just under ninety-six hours and the news
just to open an investigation. Petitions. Partitions of
I can prove it took about everything in Mary and Martha
Lazarus was indeed black and unarmed like us. Irresistible.
breath for the cost of the going rate plus interest. I have a theory.
down. Up and down, the day trades my energy for its day rays, my last
in lockstep onto a floor vast with chores and lingo that skips along. Up and
cocktails of circumstance along the way. My next steps, like bevels built to mellow,
Much like a bevy of elevator speeches uncommitted to memory, I find my words funded by

PROBABLE CAUSE

I cannot be understood in three minutes.
—Sidney Poitier

Is it just me or is this a continent of sanity I've wrought
        out of this house party? I won't fuss about it—each
 noise complaint readying to be spout, each becoming that plummets

into another log recording of our feelgood sierra as *disturbing*
        the peace—so clarify whose *peace*. All my life I've been sharp, been a black
key shunted into the peripheral. The world off-white to your liking, made in

the similitude of founding fathers bothered by the thought of us.
        Norms change by the day and dichotomy of agency I haven't yet reached.
I sing of rose water, senna, and mulberry leaves. I have no further a vantage

point to consider the fourth from. The more improbable, the more problems.
        And that's word to my stubble, my boundless biopic-to-be. And that's word to
the month of February in this, a new leap year. Vowels round as the cellulite

on me, beneath the steeple I sat. The conversations were all that and more
        as they knocked on my door. Reasonable suspicion dictates no chorus, only
a score of headlights and rap sheets. A preference of scatter, a kind of scat-

less jazz demarcating my ambush in an abandoned meadow. Surely I am
        superstitious of the cease and desist tried even the sugar in my grits. Surely you
should lower your voice when you talk at me—I warrant that. And if you say

that's reason enough to frisk me, let me get my things first. I won't be long,

    I won't be brief. The harpsichords know me well. And that's word to my glove compartment and whatever else on this fine earth you shall dust for my prints.

TWELVE

The first of my last   best memories end   in my grandma's living
room   the hushed mercury of a thermostat   the comatose

of week-old carbonated pop   and the caveat of yesterday   all bullets
are sweat   until they're not   until the sugarcoating of breath

behooves summer   I know what holiday I've taken   residence in
by the era of motown   she blasts on the stereo   if it's gladys then

autumn if it's stevie   then jubilant sky gift wrapped underneath
evergreen bristles   tonight I'm tiptoeing   around the thought of dialysis

while stars strut to temptations   and when wonder chimes in   I'll stretch
the infinity of my tissues   across the sofa's plastic   as if fragile   as if satirical

we jettison joy like a refrain rising   from the mossed floorboards up into
the attic   bypassing baby pictures   riddled with rows of teeth   I don't show

anymore   it didn't just happen overnight   there's a thin line between sorrow
and never mind   never mind I was born   with two blades in my back

///

Never mind never mind   I was born with   two blades in my back
a fistful of intent   as many arteries as there are   hours in a day
and less than half the cynicism   it takes for a white man to pray
I was born a river of vetoes   yet a river   yet a proxy for confusion

when I ask my mother   what time I came through   the function
she doesn't say anything   I ought not to know   I was born a trick
question   in budding midnight   it isn't even technically correct

to give midnight   a suffix   did you know   equidistance is another
name for   joint custody   for the fence   and the ivory one might call
neutral   even after an umbilical cord   is severed   a stump remains

after lunchtime gossip   choices   after natural disaster   disaster
and after that who knows   who's to say we can spare   the span of
this next second   to settle for rain   and call it bloom   becoming us
who's to say this world   has a long memory and forgets anyway

///

Who's to say   this world   has a long memory   and forgets   anyway
several times   I've been several feet from men   who look like me   with hands
dapping up like mine would   on the same dim-lit corners   I have been
stopped on   I've walked miles in shoes   a cop might think were theirs   check

my pockets and you'll find my signature   smudged next to a certification
that says   should the day come   the earth is in dire need   of melody and

there begins a body   ripe for a chorus but ill   a stratosphere of want   a wind
instrument   without the reservoir   lacking what   I don't lack   my organs
shall not be profiled   the same as my pigment   I've been numb   and prepared
to give   my whole life   I want the cop to know   a great deal about this

///

My whole life   I want the cop to know   a great deal about
this   the benefit of the doubt   notwithstanding

my adrenaline   infused with decades   of sentiment
not unlike preventive care   this too   a sunshine I have spent

conscious of the many   cherubs wandering among
the lushness of hoods   like mine   the pearly gates I have

paraded past   the promised lands pastured   by shepherds
I have known despite stereotypes   and prolific hypocrisies

sowed beneath our districts   the statistics of happenstance
that I   so often consider   to be a glimmer of god

in the company of martyrs   marginalized   when in fact
they did not   seek this mess   nor the messiahs   before them

///

They did not seek this mess   nor the messiahs before
them   I can attest that men learn to play men   from
men still learning   lord forgive me for the times   I
have said give me a sign   when I meant let the dark
of my eyes   see light the way a harbor can   pardon
even the most vicious tidals   ushering forth the
stench of debris   and ruin   and not call it ruined
nor name it irreparable   to the degree that there no
longer exists a good   within that body of water there
are over fifty synonyms for *body of water*   I have
found in thesauri   none of which include *heaven*
and why is that   surely there are enough bodies
that have been turned toward that coast surely there
is more than enough   good   I've lived long enough
to have seen it   be christened *sound* or *wash*   or
reservoir or   *mere* or *kill* or *run*   or *draw*   or *burn*
without mention of clouds   or gods we are said to
have been made in the image and likeness of   so say
the confessions that have come before   me saying I
asymptomatic to assumptions   of the profession of
the water   remaining a contrast   when the
hereafter meets me ashore   I'd delight in whatever
likeness the afterlife ascribes me to have been   I'd
pray it less an erosion of bronze   and more   a trail
of iridescence   more arête   and   a matter of
wavelength   than the splenetics of blues more what
seas see   post-storm in skylines vivid with the stew
of berbere and paprika   god as my witness   I'd take
anything   resembling the warmth of forgiveness

///

god   as my witness I'd take   anything resembling the warmth of forgiveness
god   as my bereavement   as my sobering   as my blackbird   as my acupuncture
god
god
god   as my overhead   as my refund   as my reprieve   as my right hand
god   as my espionage   as my inoculation   as my winterdark   as my thicket
god
god   as my dreamcatcher   as my might   as my detriment   as my palindrome
god
god   as my antioxidant   as my windpipe   as my coalition   as my crutch
god
god   as my provender   as my endeavor   as my high-rise   as my awning
god   as my silk   as my lacquer   as my protea   as my redress   as my hereditary
god
god
god   as my ontological   as my audible   as my prodigal   as my first responder
god   as my airbrush   as my amber   as my cosmos   as my candor

WHITE NOISE

That I choose love at all, that is
more honest than I care to share.

For dominoes to fall with all those
black bullets makes every sense,

as if the sum of our parts mean
our parts separate, yet equal. I can

drive daisies across state lines.
I can parallel park. But I cannot

bury the music. It trembles like
static. I took the tip of a cotton

swab to it and went too deep.
Drummed the beaten path with

words that tailed a blimp in the sky
the next day. It said, *America*

is better than this . . . mistakes
were made . . . now is the time

Reading my lips, you said this
must be a joke. How could it be

that there were those who had
rested and then there was me.

BUT WHAT'S A GOON TO A GOBLIN?

In many ways I complete America

///

Blue,
  policed

White,
  lies

Red,
  mine

///

So many times we seem to mistake our mothers for Booboo the Fool

///

I pledge

to place my hand over
my heart pumping
with promise the same

as anyone who tries
to shield their spring
from a terrible thing

THERE WILL BE TEARS

Kingdom came early last night,
brought back leftovers from
earlier. Finger foods like tuna
melts which smelled a raw

deal gone bad. *Gone too soon*
is a problem I have skipped and
skipped. Came back, too. I, like
the sight of a sun ambushed, left

my mark. *Show your work*
the sheet says for the answers
I keep fabricated in my head.
Scratch paper does me no justice

these days. During a test, look
for the penny earned and not for
the well wished. My thoughts exactly:
I knew you wouldn't believe me

so I convinced myself there was
no evidence to bring. No beauty
asleep as Aiyana before Breonna.
No breath taken from Eric before

George. When you walk right up
to her door to deliver the news,
I want you to give her this and
show her I knew of Botham,

how you can be robbed of your
life and be told *not yours*. That this
might bring the joy no me,
I make sure to carry my one.

POEM ENDING IN TWO TRUTHS AND A LIE

after Marcus Wicker

The boy was born and raised in a downward trend. On paper, it should have been as easy as giving candy to a baby, but in reality it was more like a blind date. We're talking exit strategies, subzero winters and a wealth gap where he had had the good with the bad. The nursery rhymes and the crash course. The pilot and the discontinued. How to keep up appearances and expensive taste. 1994. It was then the boy learned the price had gone up and will despite his grievances. It was then the boy recognized his quick feet, his steady bidding. *The shortest pencil is better than the longest memory.* The idea of dying for something you believe in not unlike the idea of making a name for yourself. Celebrity, celerity, sincerity, charity, clarity, or other. So the boy signed the leg of a friend of a friend cocooned in plaster. So the boy made bracelets that broke like friendship when contact contracts its destruction. So the boy was granted sneak peeks into what it is that is expendable. 1994. It was the year he learned people still lived in black and white. In the years since, the boy clung and clung to the former, glowed in the dark. No easy feat. To grind, grin, grip, gripe, grit. To spin, split, spit, sit, sift. To shun, shunt, hunt, hint, hinder. To lie, lie, lie, live, lie. It is tainted. It is impeccable. You sing *America the beautiful*, he sang *America the red flag*. You think *American*. He asks *Am i?* America, America. At its best, adjective. At its worst, adverb. The boy, yet a part of speech as tense as time.

NEVERTHELESS

When I walk into a church, I only see pictures of white angels. Why?
—Eartha Kitt

I want to take this time to focus on the timeless, as certain ones take
up arms to remove the lifetimes of those like me. My favorite word
above: a dove that sounds like I forgive myself, like a red redacted,
like a gospel according to the camaraderie I can make cousins out of.

There is no new ecclesiastical under the sun. No shortage of my people
sporting basketball shorts beneath true religion jeans. We reincarnate
every morning in these precincts with the good news delivered more
than once already. The protests of messengers sent down, the blaze

after the crossfire, a chosen people who are either a jaywalk away
from the love of our lives or our lives left to love. I have found that
the self can be its own exodus, be a black sitcom or an intercessor
for the one who waits but never goes. When I say my favorite word,

I think of how often our joy can become a win-win, how the pores of
a mother can cup holy water. Some say the world is still becoming,
but no, our angels trumpet our timbre. They are in the streets where peace
is sold separately and critique is still, policed. They stay in the cut

and on exhibit, like a glass-stained window meant to color the light.
Know we have everything in common. Nobody move. I need to
capture this moment where we are one with the unease that stomachs
us like a morning rush. How we might fill in the blank with our story,

our chalices next to paper plates, our fried and our black-eyed, our dressing, our Lawry's, our fridge tetris, and most of all, most of all, our seconds.

ALIBI IN THE MAKING

Decades from now my first father-daughter dance unrehearsed &
wouldn't you know it I'm already there though my legs are still catching
up with the most sonic parts of being present & a decade from then
decadence again sprawling over framed memories of polaroids &
wood chips beneath my new balances fortuitous & tiny as I am within
these shaky crossroad palms faced upward & after I reach a half century
Lord won't I gray into some new arrangement while cleaning afresh
collards that have minded me my nomenclature for taste *I didn't know*
you could throw down like this this is so good I want seconds & seconds if
it comes to it are precisely all I'll have to convince a barrel on another's
hip that someone along another road much flatter & less assuming than
this one did what I didn't do & seconds after that will likely feel too close
to the death of me for comfort & so much more than I care to admit I am
sure then that silhouettes will come to mind & how they were first traced
out of love for someone who was departing from a delicate ground soon
& though I'm not sure if they ever expected them to return surely time is
of the essence I belong to & so I always do & several minutes later I think
that will weigh heavily on my blood pressure because I have already in the
nightly hours prior because I plan to be on a dance floor with my loafers
sliding across a heaven of small talk & I've been told it'll feel just like
homecoming alongside a vibrant photo booth & maybe music I have
heard before & a fond orchestra of heraldic balloons guarding the
windexed doors & splendid thin ribbons reeling into the helium of me

UNTITLED MEDLEY

Oh, I think they like me
with a brain freeze,

my sneeze summered into
sensations: showmanship.

Oh, I think they like
me down with the power
moves and painkillers,

circa my shoddy stint
as somebody's son.

Direct deposits with my name
cursed along their backs

and mine along a muted seat
I paid good money for.
Oh, I think they like me with my

towering spine, my uneven
hips, my enamel as dark as the sense

of humor on my mother's side.
I'd rather the route of washing

a mouth out with black soap
than my father's
slapping *the black off me*,

and I think they like me
like that: with the black off.

Oh, I think they like me in
a fugitive color—

indigo lake, carmine, or
rose madder. It gets
to me how these

fighting words warm
me with their blue

bias, warn me of my
stingy gestures

grandfathered in.
Lightfast after I lift
a mirror to my eye

level and spot a taper
as timid as tough love.

Oh, I think they
like me for it: my MO,

who I am when I am
laid off, my stunt double
and inside voice

careening about.

I WANT ALL THE SMOKE

but so does the sky. Most don't make it past the first line yet
       here we are. Once I tell you what happens next,

       there's no turning back. Across from me, Garfield Park

beholden to preteens on gravitating swing sets. At that age, you wake up
       with no dilemmas and fall asleep expecting much less.

       Darkness cannot get named after your despair

until you first experience your own laws of motion. Mine, self-serving,
       after static stifled my legs to the degree

       that I could even start to consider what betrayal looks like.

That the backstabbers the O'Jays told us to watch out for may very well
       pale in comparison to our own blood rushed.

       How does one look for a fight when it is already in you?

I fear I've misjudged my capacity to the degree that I am exempt.
       Even after I infuse imperatives into

       my statements, they end up the least of my doing.

Lend me a flash of brilliance that isn't a siren. Lend me an aurora
       that isn't a clearing. I need the cop

to apprehend, I've cried before without relapse

or the seduction of tear gas. I don't need you to coax it out of me.
My ancestors have already lifted my voice through song.

Just say the word and I can take a polygraph

whenever you'd like. The notes are no different than every day you have
written, than each sunrise which needed the night before.

You know, I haven't the slightest idea why you assume I want

what I won't handle. It's almost as if I open my mouth and you forget, then
remember how I've been denied the lands

I've once watered, how once, once I was the glory.

FORTE

You can't hold the record forever, and I know that. I'm not stupid.
—Janet Jackson

SERENDIPITY

Potent as an exhale, I am telling you
I don't need good luck to make riddance

of any unrequited bounty. I am more than I intended to be,
which is to say I acquired the taste of things hoped for

on accident. As a result, I made a mannerism out of faith, out of
picking up disposed petals like one would a jewel. There is no

greater love than that which becomes of us after we are on our knees.
Bunny-eared shoelaces or a proposal. Speaking of which, I have

chiseled one to sing. Of which, I'll concede that when I do question
what it means to be sacred, I suppose that is my funny way of asking

about even the softest parts of me which have been grazed through
the years. I suppose I am not ashamed of my mistakes the same way

a body is humbled by the dirt that sticks, the flagrant dents indulging,
the auspicious spine healing. Its palmy preservation just as slick

as a squad. How when I say squad, I mean gang. How when
I say gang, I mean psalms so sharp with mercy it is becoming

harder for me to neglect how suds want nothing more than for
our bodies to ask them to stay the night, how romantic would that be.

SOMETIMES I FORGET TO SAY GRACE

You have been here
before. The bread
baking, then breaking,
then. A second wind.
The evening evening
out over the squeeze

of hunched shoulders.
The batter in the bellies
of those who think
the Lord implied.
What's understood
doesn't need to be

explained, but what
have you done with
your five loaves lately?

Nothing,
I have multiplied
nothing

but my restlessness.
I am in the business
of brisk surrenders
and blindfolds I can
unhand if and where
I see fit. The perfect

crime is the one
in which no one is
caught fidgeting with
the foil. I am not keen
on taking down
my own statements

but I do so after
I get a snoop at my want.
And the heat rises.

SELF-PORTRAIT WITH WAVE GREASE

Sometimes exodus precedes genesis
and shallow ends are born premature

to this world without the bandwidth
to nourish. My favorite version

of a nightcap involves my naps neat
as clutter, kicking a flutter that swells

to keep us afloat. When I must breathe,
it is viral for good reason. Skin turned

blue in the night is kin, bearing the news
of its bad, blues to the light. The heaviest

hues are held tight with the right to remain.
Aboveground and below, a matter of life

in graves. I only have but one direction: brush
until the price of my slice of pie leaves me

fuller. Roll tide into the perfect dark dreams are
made of. When we get there, I'll let you know.

THE MUSIC OF BEING YOUNG AND DUMB

Young, we were the epitome of fatigue
and the boast of blisters. Balloons
botched by our nimble fingers, we

bragged with chapped lips. We sipped
through gaps and dwelled in the garden
of ease. Frivolous was our fortune.

A second nature, where we deemed discretion
unnecessary. We did not want. My, how gentle
it was in the valleys where we went to vanish.

It took the glue of a village to rile us in,
craft and rope lapping our rebellion
like a modest fence. However unconscionable

it seemed, we sidestepped when they dubbed
our imaginations illegitimate. Still do. We went
over this already. There's homesick and then

there's home sick. There's the space granted
and then there's the rigged recusal. The limit
to our love? Same difference. Replacing the flinty

rope around our necks with stoles. Our joys
redundant, chapters upon the storied in one
hand and in the other, freezer-burned ice cream.

To cherish and be cherished. I don't feel the need
to explain much more to you because we
wrote this book. Excuse us, coming through.

Excuse us, excuse us, it's time to shine.

SELF-PORTRAIT IN LIEU OF MY EP

Nobody step to me unless they got a problem with the way I cradle the mic because I cradle the mic my way. Nobody gets to question what I feel. Everybody's fluent in silence. I feel like I am still waiting to come in. When I speak and the tables have turned, I think of turntables. When the beat drops, I let you tell it though I've already talked that talk. It's like that. On my résumé, action verbs. In my coffee, a black I recognize even after adding more sugar. In the plastic-sheathed rectangles of our most revisited photo album, a djembe I played like there was a stop made for me on the soul train line. Second cousin to the sun so it's a cookout every time I walk outside. And a reunion for each new dance my brothers and sisters make before I wake up and learn its choreo. It's like that. And it has been since I found the progression from A minor to G major. And it has been since I froze on the two like a mannequin. Since the upbeat of my pulse had a plus-one added to its thump. Baby, since self-interest. Since backwash. Since way back. Since carburetors mixed fuel with the referendum of air. Car don't got no roof. It's like that. Like that very first taste of hypocrisy, the fetal position practiced and fittingly forgotten when the speakers pick me up with my filth. The things I've brag-rapped on tempo, a magna carta barter I can call a track if I run fast enough for you to ignore what we've kept a hundred. I've said what I said and now a bridge where I can check the one-two thrice before twelve hit a U-turn. Before it's all sirens and hoping those lights pass me by. It's like that.

WHIPLASH

I was near death,
and then I wasn't. We
had a falling out, my bumper
took the brunt of the hit from the
errant Cadillac. But I was the fall guy

beyond the tardy heuristic. A plaintiff proximate
to the fault when the cop needed to know where I had been
at the full stop, why I had not fit the profile, profound *at the mercy of*.

It felt like the hottest day on earth when I stepped out of the car, all my limbs

intact and miserable. The asphalt a grade below, the airbag a lousy
confidant, the night sweats coming to pass like a sick, tacky
quip at autocorrect. The world wanted me to fathom

how lucky I was. The ferocious fluke of my
neck, my back. My word. Waiting to
talk seemed a lot like waiting to
exhale that night and the
morning was just that.

MURPHY'S LAW

To be a fighter is to be
a lover I learn this like

a passenger who cannot
choose between saying

I told you so and letting it
go. Countless are the words

I cannot think to use when
I am cut off in traffic. Aimless

is the sound let loose in a car
in which the stereo is hushed,

the light gleams emerald, and
the wheel yields to the you who

has yet to choose which exit is next.
Did you miss it? *I told you so.*

To be a lover is to be a fighter
and I know this by my show

of hands, suspended like an aria
when we realize we are neither.

ABRACADABRA ALL THE SADDER

While the dew is still on the roses, shut-eye and halls opening up
my throat for the sob I segue into. Never mind the drip on my knockoff

flip-flops or the right-of-way ceded to the proceeding hearses before us,
I am reminded of the sunroof I hardly ever open. What's a light fixture

to a deity, a throne for the one who does not want it. Like the middle seat
in a carpool, what restrains us is that which we've deemed unbearable

and that precisely is what contrives a tomb. Question: where is it
you've placed the teleprompter with the words I haven't yet found

for the catastrophes searing this world? In the dream recurring to my
dismay, I wake to run my hand beneath a vine of tap water. I am most

concerned by the optics of it all. How to debone chicken, how I separate
my dark from my light before I arrive to the laundromat, how to somersault,

how not to manufacture moonshine, how to pose for someone who's pressing
a button while they tell you of your need to relax, how cherry blossoms bring out

my eyes, and how the whites of another's are turning yellow while their liver
shuts down. Lucky for me, I've never had to know what it is to tonic

a lamentation like one would as they cremate a body they've once loved.
I don't want to discern this alone. Don't tell me where you're from, tell me

where you want to get to. Tell me you, too, pull over when you see the white
flags on antennas of automobiles waving for those of us still searching

for grounds which are suitable enough for our dead. Tell me the chai
you'd suggest to somebody like me who has grown tired of the lukewarm.

Where have you gone that makes it feel like night and day? Reception
out here's terrible, and I need a spot with plenty of legroom.

WHEN I FEEL WHAT I FEEL

after Morgan Parker

Language back then was all over the place,
a rotary phone with my pinkie pent up, reaching

more or less for a connection. *Less is more—*
lip service for my kind of kindness. So when

I give you my word, I am perhaps giving you
a discarded stem. A bad apple and its few

good seeds. I pick logs out of my eye like fruits
of your labor. Look at my core. I would like to

appreciate you the way you want to be appreciated.
A nod from afar is a love language to some and

that's fine. What's not is how I get the timing
wrong. On the screen, the home team runs
their two-minute drill and still doesn't score.

Doesn't get the snap off in time. When asked *why*
in the interview, coach says he doesn't know but

the clock is in the same place it's always been. It takes
no time to get on the same page. Tonight,

when I said *I'm ready*, we had two diverging trains
of thought. You thought it'd be another twenty

minutes, I considered whether the future
perfect would have been *will have been ready* or *will*

have to be ready. I don't know the difference and
utter *let's table this for the train* to your surprise.

PARABLE FULL OF FIRSTS

Jesus wept, while at the altar watching
his favorite people wed. Not by sight, but by
the element of surprise. Sheets of rain
like linen or cake stomped the turf like

a trouble he knew well. Alpha and Omega gave
toasts, were so drunk that no one could grasp
what they had said. Each emotion was
seconded that night, as they listened to one-
hit wonders and warped their speech
through liquid vows and hiccups. The first
dance was more of a mess than anyone
could've predicted. Sloppy copies of themselves

as the music took them for a test drive.
If you can believe it, everyone had to drive
stick shift home or catch a ride with
a stranger savvy enough to sift through stop

signs. Thankfully, there were no accidents, only
mortal commandments sent like *did you make it*
home safely or *I'd rather you stay over than*
end up somewhere you couldn't start fresh from.
The next morning, everything felt new and due
like jury duty, or mixed signals. Like the point
of no return, but with a softness like
that of a cushion. Like the gap a baby's tooth

dreams up when it departs—an endeavor
toward a gift of trust. All they could talk about
was the rehearsal dinner and the brown
snowfall that miracled and speckled after they

scrubbed butter onto bread burned but soaked
in what abided. I remember. It was on a Tuesday.
They were all making their way to Wednesday
with to-dos piling up for Thursday.

They were not even on Friday's mind.
But everyone was in love. Everyone was in love.

LIKE A MILLION SUNSETS ON BOOTLEG

You had me at daylight savings,
at the risk of sounding too high-

      maintenance. You had me at matinée,
      how fleeting was a way to chronicle

            the drapes, rays, and our looming
            insurrection. If you must know,

      it wasn't glamorous when I was yours
      truly for the first time. That winter was

full of antics and keepsakes—the swindle
of child lock and of wanting to escape to

      nowhere better. You had me at foolproof,
      though those weren't the words we used.

            Honestly, half the time words weren't that
            at all. Seemed like hints at nutrition, from

      here, like sparks off the tips of a bonfire,
      the splendor of s'mores and carnival funnel

cake. You had me at *for real*, as in the hours
we spent flabbergasted during scenes where

      our desires felt derivative. Our bewilderment
      so in sync we'd linger there in the pitch black,

after the credits had scrolled their way
back to the clouds our minds were last.

MANY HANDS MAKE LIGHT

Last night, the rest was history. We were thriving in the stuffiest circulation a summer house had to offer. We were watching the sixth episode of season four for the ninth time at a banquet, the bread near the centerpiece growing cold as we continued to fumble with the volume beneath the white tablecloth. We were spotting the concealed gats and turning away from what we couldn't bear to see. We were gasping for room-temperature air uttering the words *I told you so, I told you so* and daring anyone at all to knock on wood. We were velvet-voiced and instantaneously changing our minds about PDA and the perks of doing crosswords next to someone who had already finished your sentences for you several times before. We were laughing off stage fright. We were outside the chapel gawkily playing miss mary mack when I wasn't so flustered to fail in front of boys apathetic to learning how. We were walking out of rooms with our backs facing forward, our hands lifted like a surgeon's in sterile territory. We were plotting the upside of heading to Kroger to grab some cookie dough and then we weren't. We were deliberating all of what we could make from scratch.

IN PRAISE OF PROTECTIVE STYLES

I imagine how difficult it must be to give *the talk* in a nest where
    ends were made to meet. In the ends where the usual
    suspects—cottonmouth, lockjaw, tragedy at first
    sight—assume the quiet as a kind of cosmology

in certain households like mine. Jeopardy on the line. Détente.
    And I am reminded of what is for show and what
    I can tell. *Please hold*, and I am caught hoarding
    my news like I was taught. This is what I know:

defensive driving in a midwestern rush hour. Traveling light
    on backstreets. Preemptive escape plans for every
    room I walk into. How when my mother says
    because I said so and *when you grow older, you'll*

understand why, I believe in the talks that she has cocooned inside her
    throat. How I trust a lens limited is still a lens infinite.
    That there could be rage behind the scope of a rifle
    is sure enough to make me believe in the sage

behind lucrative counsel. Before I know it, it has been too long and I
    hear her yelling from the other room to hang up and call
    back later. Naturally in the distance, more aphorisms at
    too low a level. I respond *hold on* like I can afford to.

THE CONCEPT OF SCHOOL
SEEMS SO SECURE

For every palm, there is a Sunday, and for every crown, a crown
　　　spared the plight of something precious. Stability,
　　　so long as we call it such, spins into stipends.

Homies shout *secure the bag* as if the grind isn't liable for
　　　our muscle memory thrush with burnout. Must
　　　I skip a grade to pave this road of grave

intentions? Must authority be that which the lips lock but never
　　　let go of? Packing my north face full of felled fibers
　　　is not unlike stress or the small truths we concede

to make room for smaller ones. Heavy are the hands begetting
　　　said casualties and heavy also are the many pupils
　　　dilated for what little light has yet to single file

in the name of day care. All this refuge is of no use if I am half-
　　　handed in my show-and-tell of decency. I am still
　　　learning my faults, the closures I chose.

Somewhere, a wage is a wage is a wage, each partitioned into a trivia,
　　　small enough to spoon and preface a child's first words.
　　　And not one cites taxes or tombs. Not one.

ON CUE

after Etheridge Knight

And now that the sun is going,
going, going, gone. Dawn, lolling
around looking larger than life.

The nine-year-old boy in me knows
the adage: *if you're early, you're on
time, and if you're on time, you're late.*

So the boy now knows the nerve of saviors.
Maybe the nerve of never. How the day
goes just how the day comes. Somewhere,

someone is punching the clock so the boy
can dispose of dust and rinse away some
more earth in a new light. A slippery trope.

Create in me a clean heart, the boy recites,
and renew a right spirit within me. Years
later, only now a renewal of his temple—

the end of his lease. So here it is: head
bowed, eyes closed. The least I could
do. Prayer as a hail mary, a last-ditch

effort albeit with a corroded shovel.
When paying my respects in this way,
I choose to leave behind begonias to keep

the weeds company. My relationship to faith
faltering. Locked knees and asking
who's there like a terrible knock-knock joke

without a clue of what's coming. When I look
up all I see are angels, and think this
must be the perfect time for a trust fall.

Notes

"When I Feel What I Feel" is written in response to and after Morgan Parker's "Black Ego (Original Soundtrack)" in *Magical Negro*.

"On Cue" is written in response to and after Etheridge Knight's "The Sun Came" in *The Essential Etheridge Knight*, which is inspired by and in conversation with Gwendolyn Brooks's poem "Truth" in *Blacks*.

"Self-Portrait in Lieu of My EP" borrows a line from Douglas Manuel's "Loud Looks" in *Testify*.

"Men Like Me" references a tweet by Kiese Laymon on August 22, 2018, regarding accountability in the face of terror brought on by patriarchal violence.

"Small Devotionals" is written in response to and after Ladan Osman's "Devotional with Misheard Lyrics" in *Exiles of Eden*.

"Poem Ending in Two Truths and a Lie" is written in response to and after Marcus Wicker's "Interrupting Aubade Ending in Epiphany" in *Maybe the Saddest Thing*.

"Concerning Social Security" is written in response to and after Yona Harvey's "The Subject of Retreat" in *You Don't Have to Go to Mars for Love*.

"*I Don't Get Dropped, I Drop the Label*" takes its title from a line written in the song "On to the Next One" by Jay-Z and Swizz Beatz on the album *The Blueprint 3*.

"*The Concept of School Seems So Secure*" takes its title from a line written in the song "All Falls Down" by Kanye West and Syleena Johnson on the album *The College Dropout*.

"*Abracadabra All the Sadder*" takes its title from a line written in the song "Ms. Jackson" by OutKast on the album *Stankonia*.

"Lessons from Cooley High" takes its title in reference to *Cooley High*, a movie released in 1975 on the day and life of black teenagers in Chicago and is a call-and-response to the character Preach (played by Glynn Turman).

"There Is No I in Denial" reflects on a scene featuring Dwayne Wayne (portrayed by Kadeem Hardison) in episode 25, season 5 ("Save the Best for Last, Pt. 2") of the television series *A Different World*.

"*The Music of Being Young and Dumb*" takes its title from a line in the song "Sherane a.k.a. Master Splinter's Daughter" by Kendrick Lamar on the album *good kid, m.A.A.d city*.

"*But What's a Goon to a Goblin?*" takes its title from a line written in the song "A Milli" by Lil' Wayne on the album *Tha Carter III*.

"*I Know the Hustle So Well*" takes its title from a line written in the song "Lord Knows" by Drake and Rick Ross on the album *Take Care*.

Acknowledgments

If it isn't clear yet, I am still on my way. This book was made possible by the very blessing of being pushed and enveloped. For that I am truly grateful. I would like to thank a few special folks who I am indebted to for their invaluable support:

An eternal thank you to my wife, my better heart and light in love, Audrianna, for being my delight. Thank you for the marvelous ways you preserve wonder and for continuing to cherish us in such a brilliant manner. I love you.

Deep gratitude to my community—Kim, Olatunbosun, Olajuwon, Walterine, Annie, Akintunde, Peter, Kenneth, Reginald, Kimberly, Derek, Alexandria, Atayliya, Ava, LaToya, Phyllis, and the extended family. Thank you for your remarkable love and guidance.

Gratitude to the crew who kept me true in the creation of this book: Bryan Byrdlong, Josh Everett, Daniel Anderson, Kheri Dunkins, Al Hardaway, Jasmine Arrington, Maggie Bates, Zach Williams, Zipporah Champion, Yelana Sims, Brandan Gillespie, Lauren Saxon, Moose Song, Austin Paramore, James Zhang, Ronald Lewis Jr., and Tariq Simpkins.

Thank you to the many journals and publications that first welcomed and tended to versions of these poems as this quilt of a book came together: *Southeast Review*, *Tinderbox*, *Wildness*, *Cosmonauts Avenue*, *Bodega*, *Prelude*, *Frontier Poetry*, *RHINO*, *Split This Rock*, *Backbone Press*, *Palette Poetry*, and the *Best New Poets* anthology.

Deep thanks to Camille Rankine, for seeing this book and selecting it for such an honor as this. To Daniel Halpern, Beth Dial, and the NPS team, thank you. To Johnny Temple and the Akashic family, thank you for your sensational editorial vision and for making this book a reality.

Lastly, thank you to Chicago, my city. The West Side I carry with me daily. Thank you to the world around me and its nearing moment full of life yet lived. I'll be with you soon.

Originally from the West Side of Chicago, **Olatunde Osinaike** is a Nigerian American poet and software developer. He is the winner of the Lucille Clifton Poetry Prize, a Frontier Poetry Industry Prize, and honorable mention for the *Ploughshares* Emerging Writer's Award in Poetry. His work has appeared in *Best New Poets*, *New Poetry from the Midwest*, *Kweli Journal*, *Wildness*, *Southeast Review*, and elsewhere. He lives in Atlanta.

Printed in the USA
CPSIA information can be obtained
at www.ICGtesting.com
CBHW030341191223
2696CB00006B/29